Back to School @30

Back to School @30

Rashmi Singh

Publishers
Pustak Mahal®

J-3/16 , Daryaganj, New Delhi-110002
☎ 23276539, 23272783, 23272784 • *Fax:* 011-23260518
E-mail: info@pustakmahal.com • *Website:* www.pustakmahal.com

Sales Centre

- 10-B, Netaji Subhash Marg, Daryaganj, New Delhi-110002
  ☎ 23268292, 23268293, 23279900 • *Fax:* 011-23280567
  E-mail: rapidexdelhi@indiatimes.com
- 6686, Khari Baoli, Delhi-110006
  ☎ 23944314, 23911979

Branches

Bengaluru: ☎ 080-22234025 • *Telefax:* 080-22240209
E-mail: pustak@airtelmail.in • pustak@sancharnet.in
Mumbai: ☎ 022-22010941, 022-22053387
E-mail: rapidex@bom5.vsnl.net.in
Patna: ☎ 0612-3294193 • *Telefax:* 0612-2302719
E-mail: rapidexptn@rediffmail.com
Hyderabad: *Telefax:* 040-24737290
E-mail: pustakmahalhyd@yahoo.co.in

ISBN 978-81-223-1367-3

Edition: 2012

Printed at : Param Offsetters, Okhla, Delhi

Reviews

Praise for previous work: Taming the Restless Mind

Book Chums, a Community of book lovers says 'People dealing with confidence and self-development issues must give it a read. There are many winning tricks highlighted in the book that are bound to help readers gather and uplift their self-esteem and decision making skills.

I will suggest this book to youngsters definitely so that they are at least aware of the things that they are doing wrong (yes, already) and how they can improve their communication and interpersonal skills, as they stand on the brink of the transition (from a youngster to an adult)'.

http://soniareviews.wordpress.com/2012/02/13/book-review-of-taming-the-restless-mind-by-rashmi-singh/

Anuradha Shankar I.G.P. Indore says, 'Rashmi has really excelled in bringing out the day to day problems of the youth. In fact I hope with this kind of guidance, the youth today is surely going to benefit. Proud of the author'.

Dr Ranju Singh, Psychiatrist and Retd. Principal, Anganbadi says 'This book will surely help the youngsters to find the right path of life. It will show the girls and boys both, the correct path and how to safe guard themselves from the accruing rave parties and late night dating'.

Amod Kumar, IES, DOT says, 'Many topics in this valuable book are invaluable. We all know them but we do not apply them in our lives. This book has in a very simple way showed us the ways to actually apply and follow them in our day to day life'.

Acknowledgements

My beloved parents twinkling amongst the stars, D P Singh & Shanti Devi, for instilling in me the mettle of a 'fighter' …

My father-in-law B N Singh & mother-in-law Prem Lata Singh.

My lovely children, Apurva and Ayushree for always cheering me up.

My husband, Amod Kumar.

My sister-in-law, Anita Singh for pushing me ahead on the path of life.

My brother, Sunil Kumar Singh for his unconditional love and support.

Sister Mary Beena, Notre Dame Academy, Patna, for enlightening my path of life.

Tejrashi Mehrotra ma'am, for supporting me 'since my blogging days'.

My students, friends & sisters especially Dr. Nisha Singh with her motherly warmth.

My 'faith' and 'self perseverance' for always staying by my side.

Mr Rohit Gupta, CEO, **Pustak Mahal** for having immense and unquestionable faith in me and my work.

And above all – GOD!

Special Thanks:

Dr V.K. Goel and his team, Sai Hospital, Moradabad.

Dr Neeraj Gupta, Senior Psychiatrist, Chetna Clinic, Moradabad.

Dr Avinash Kumar Singh, Retired C.M.O. Motihari.

Dr Arvind Minz, Senior Consultant, QRG Hospital Faridabad.

Dr Ranju Singh, Psychiatrist and Retired Principal, 'Anganbadi', Muzaffarpur.

AUTHOR'S NOTE:

During my long tenure as Personality Development Trainer and Counsellor, I have sincerely felt that Personality Polishing is not only required by students or those trying to get jobs. It is one important ingredient of life required at almost all stages of development and especially by those trying to make their journey smooth in the rugged path of life in their thirties and beyond.

Almost two decades back people in their thirties had a feeling of warmth, compassion and generosity about them. They were not too ambitious and were almost content with their meager incomes but with drastic changes in life style, values and education patterns, 'thirties' has become the most tender period of life requiring extreme care. It is this period where men /women face their major challenges and the conflicts that arise due to this are sometimes extreme.

Work culture, social values, financial stability, all have added immense pressure on people of this age ruining their emotional stability and conscientiousness – making them rude, callous and rash to the extent that they unknowingly march towards the grip of the deadly monster 'DEPRESSION'!

It is at this age a need arises, that 'they be sent back to some kind of classroom to hone, polish and discipline their lives and personality'. It is here 'they' must check this cancerous growth on their lives or else life ahead could be fatal.

'Back to School @30' is written for men and women in their thirties and beyond, struggling with their lives. Men and women who are trying not only to make big but who are also reorganizing their relationships!

In fact while trying to make big, they forget the basic disciplines, once taught to them in schools. This book is going to make them realize about those aspects of their lives which they have completely ruined and need to pay attention to before they reach the dead end of the road.

This book will help people beyond the age of thirty to look beyond the Simple Solution of Punishment. We all wish for a psychological pain reliever to relieve our worries and pains. We would like someone else to solve the problem of violence in our society. We want the police, the courts, and the prisons to do their jobs and to protect us from criminals. What we do not actually realize is that it is 'WE' who are creating this ruckus and it is only 'WE' who can solve this. We forget that, there is one area where we can influence aggressive behaviour; that is to learn how to control our own counter aggressive actions.

This book will finally make people aware about the loopholes, the decaying areas of life which should be 'schooled, tamed and channelized' to improve and foster their physical-mental health and relationships.

For any query contact:

rrashmi211@gmail.com

https://www.facebook.com/Rashmii.S

PREFACE

"Mommie, Ritu has snatched my candy," five-year-old Raju was yelling at the top of his voice.

"Doesn't matter beta, I will get another one for you," Raju's mom tried to pacify him.

"Noooooo, I want the one she has snatched from me," a vociferous Raju made his mother's life hell. Meanwhile Ritu was nowhere to be found. The six-year-old girl had already absconded with her precious 'loot'. The day was Sunday, and Raju's mother was already messed up as her cook had stayed away from coming. She had to do important official work as well and now the unbelievable fight after a 'silly candy' infuriated her. Getting thoroughly irritated, she slapped the boy hard and in seconds was lamenting her act.

The above incident can be acceptable, as those bickering over a candy were innocent children. But what would happen, if grownups fight over such petty issues and consequently end up being chided in the manner Raju was! Wouldn't the scene be funny, hilarious and unbelievable? But most often it is this dark humour that makes our lives miserable! So let us dive into this book and read the complex situations which the people in their thirties and beyond face or we can say rather create. A sincere effort has been made to provide solutions to such awkward situations.

'So what makes a healthy personality?'

Psychologists have been studying this important question and have come to the conclusion that in humans, personality comprises of the 'BIG FIVES'. Broad consensus today is that personality traits are best described by the "Big Fives": **Extraversion, Agreeableness, Conscientiousness, Emotional stability,** and **Openness** to experience and at least two of these five traits appear to be directly related to physical well-being and longevity: Emotional stability and Conscientiousness.

More to the point, wellness is linked to changes in these traits over time. Sometimes these 'big fives' are broken into smaller characteristics determining our personality. When you think of someone as "steady" or "flaky" or "gloomy" or "daring," what you're really doing is unconsciously taking a measure of these five traits and crunching them together.

The book is a genuine approach to provide a peep into the life and characteristics of this 'sensitive' age group to understand where they are exactly drifting and how they can stabilize their lives, creating a better environment for themselves, society and a yet more candid approach to better their relationships.

Contents

Chapter One

Parent-Child Ruinous Rivalry

Rivalry in relationships: are you jealous of your own sibling's, spouse's, children's, achievements and personality?

I've always believed that 'age is just a number'. Some people agree with me; a lot of people don't – depending on our upbringing, cultural background and even our religion. But recently I have realized age is not just a number! It does take a toll on our personality, social and personal life. And if we have to make it just 'a number' then we have to channelize our relationships in such a way, that with every passing day we find a reason to clap for ourselves..

Everyone experiences a tinge of jealousy every now and then. It is totally a natural feeling. While no one will ever completely get over feeling the pangs of jealousy since it is a universal emotion, some people manage to quickly get over it, work past it, or control it. This is an important thing to do so that self doubt does not adversely affect them in the long run, or lead to a major depression or even violence. But if this green-eyed monster becomes unhealthy and stings your relationships, it is high time you waken your senses!

Here is a true story narrated by a lady whom I came across in my counselling sessions. She was direly upset with her husband's behaviour.

REASON: Her husband always wanted the same t-shirt with the same design which her teenage son used to buy for himself. The situation worsened when her husband started stealing his son's clothes and desperately tried to fit into them, and in attempting so, ruined them completely. Just read:

"Hello Rashmi."

"Hello Punam. How are you? Oh My God, you are looking haggard! What's the matter?" I asked the thoroughly upset lady.

"Actually I am upset with my husband's behaviour!" Teary-eyed, she looked at me totally emaciated.

"Why? What's the matter?" I gave her a suspicious look, quite taken aback by her depressed and thwarted self. It was either '*Alcohol*' or '*Another Woman*' as these two seemed the most plausible reasons to me.

"Oh! He has become so obnoxious!" She continued in a fidgety state. "He wants to wear almost the same kind of attire which my eighteen-year-old son does. Sometimes, when my son Anuj is not around, he rummages his wardrobe, picks up few funky shirts and tries them out and even walks out wearing them down to the market! He looks weird in them but doesn't listen to anyone. In fact Anuj tried to reason out with his father but his reasoning fell deaf on his father's ears!" She lamented and said in a go, panting and gulping water down her parched throat as if trying to pacify her anxious mind!

"Oh! So this is the matter?" I said giving an assuring look and smiling at her to soothe her worried mind but at the same time knowing very well that the father here was getting jealous of his own son's personality and this burgeoning insecurity is making him jealous of his own child.

“But Rashmi, don’t you think it is alarming?” she inquired still panting.

“Yes Punam, it is alarming and you have come to me at the right time!” I said with deep frowns.

“So now..?” she questioned frantically.

“So, now what? It’s nothing. This is very common. Even mothers sometimes get jealous of their teenage daughter’s beauty or achievements.” I said reflectively.

“But I am not…,” said Punam slowly.

“Maybe, you are not. But generally it happens and sometimes daughters too don’t like their mothers to dress up as they feel insecure – they feel their mothers are walking away with all attention which in fact they should have got!” I said looking into her eyes.

“Ohhh!” But tell me what do I do now? My son is gruesomely upset and wants to stay with a paying guest and this would be a matter of shame for me and my family!” she said almost sobbing.

“Listen Punam,” I said determinedly. “It is a very common problem and there’s nothing to panic about. Actually now that you have realized your husband’s folly, you have to bear up with it. First of all you have to make your son realize that his father is undergoing hormonal changes and hence the insecurity. It is not always the woman who faces the negative consequences of hormonal changes". I continued and sat with her for almost an hour, discussing her problem and suggesting her ways to combat her fear.

Almost after one month she rang me up informing that her husband is no more trying out his hands on his son's shirts and wardrobe as she is buying some like dresses for him! And all the while she is continuously making him aware that he, as a matter of fact doesn't look good in them. The

result: Her husband Mohan Kumar had finally reconciled to his state and age and matured into a 55 years old man!

In the above case, we conclude that it was close to a case of Jealousy.

Here are some tips to stop being so jealous.

Acknowledge That You Are Jealous

Try to figure out the reasons for your self-doubt. Often, if you can identify the root cause of what is triggering the jealousy and self-doubt, then you can try to get past it. Some people are jealous because of a feeling of entitlement. You may be jealous of their big house and expensive car. However, unless they were born rich, they would probably tell you how hard they have worked to earn this and the sacrifices they made to achieve success, such as restricted time for children or several failed marriages. Money and success do not always translate into happiness.

Stop Comparing Yourself to Others

Everyone needs to have their own dreams and goals. Then they need to concentrate on achieving those goals, rather than comparing themselves to others. Self-doubt can take over if you let it. So remind yourself that you are a different person.

Other People's Issue of Self-Doubt

When you encounter someone who is bragging and showing off, which is making you jealous, realize that they may be acting this way out of their own self-doubts and low self-esteem. They are building themselves up in your mind in an attempt to get your approval. Often, these people have a very low self-esteem and need to belittle others to make themselves feel better. Instead of feeling jealous, turn it into pity for those people.

Learn From the Success of Others

Instead of being jealous, turn that self-doubt around and learn what has made them a success and utilize some of those things for yourself. Turn that jealousy into constructive action and use it as motivation to achieve your own goals, dreams and desires.

Change Your Attitude

Take responsibility for your own actions and the resulting consequences. Be persistent in achieving your own goals. When you feel self-doubt creeping up, just remember that you are not in competition with the world. Use self-doubt as a tool for improvement. The journey is often more important than the final outcome.

List Reasons Why Others Should Be Jealous Of You

Concentrate on your own success and achievements, as well as the things, people or pets that bring you joy.

Stop underestimating yourself and putting yourself down. Many people are just as jealous of you as you are of them. However, you are too busy experiencing self-doubt that you do not realize it. Stand tall in your own success and achievements. You are a wonderful person.

⁂⁂

Chapter Two

THIRTY PLUS SYNDROME

Manipulative Parents: A Pain In The Neck

Signs of a Manipulative Parent

Sometimes Parents in guise of a 'Controlling Parent' actually turn out to be manipulative and jealous. Let's check:

There is a lot of similarity between a manipulative parent and a controlling parent. However, controlling parents are obvious in their actions and say things as they are.

Manipulative parents on the other hand, are likely to twist words to elicit an action or a response from their children. Some of the common traits of manipulative parents include:

* Behaving like victimized individuals whose world only consists of misery
* Indirectly blaming their children for their condition
* Eliciting guilt via emotional blackmailing
* Exploiting weaknesses in children to make them feel guilty
* Underlying aggressive personality, the traits of which are seen in the aforementioned manner
* Interfering with every aspect of a child's life so as to have some amount of control on her/him
* Forcing children to do things for them that they would not willingly do
* Discouraging children's endeavours by discarding them as impossible or wild
* Shirking personal responsibility in order to avoid accusations
* Discouraging discussion on facts that may indicate personal responsibility for their situation

It is important to understand that manipulative parents are trying to prevent the occurrence of certain situations rather than dealing with them. They simply do not want to accept that they may be responsible for their own condition. Why do manipulative parents behave in this manner? Sometimes, it is because they themselves have grown up in an environment like that, which is why as a child of a manipulative parent, you should be careful that it does not rub off on you.

Believe it or not, some parents are jealous of their children's achievements.

While it is a stated fact that parents always want the best for their children, some cannot tolerate it. Some believe that if they could not go that far, they will not allow their children to do it either. These heightened insecurities may be subconscious but may show in conscious action. Manipulation also gives a strong sense of control that some parents truly enjoy. As mentioned earlier, controlling parents are explicit, but manipulative parents are a little subtle in comparison. Finally, some parents just like being victims of misery. They enjoy the attention that being in pain brings them, which is when they begin to put themselves in such situations so that you run to their rescue.

When was the last time you kissed your children goodnight?

It is well said "A kiss without a hug is like a flower without the fragrance".

And kisses are not only meant for lovers or beloved. A kiss holds a great importance for children as well. Although children grow up into mature adults, they still want their parents to connect with them, pamper them, in spite of the age factor.

My son, Apurva, twenty-two years old, is a graduate engineer and is currently placed with a renowned company but still when he comes back from his work at night, he wants me to be around – to kiss him on his forehead when he is dozing off to sleep and oil his hair. These little gestures of affection keep us connected. Children as they grow up are faced with numerous career choices – choices that might compel them to change their city/country base and settle abroad, but the emotional bond is one such factor that mocks at the distance.

My sixteen-year-old daughter Ayushree too, now and then, yearns for a 'hug' and a 'kiss'. Whenever I accidentally bend towards her, while she is sitting and studying, she looks up to me anticipating a hug. If I fail to understand this and start doing some other work, she pulls up a long face. Gradually I have tried to understand her needs and concerns.

Pamper them, in spite of the age factor

I tried discussing this with her and she agreed that she wants to be loved and caressed even though she is considered 'a grown up' by most. And now I am often hugging her.

But your child may not necessarily be like her. They might even hate discussing this with their parents. This doesn't mean they do not want to be loved. It is just like their parents; they too are undergoing massive hormonal changes and are not able to accept what they want! So parents, if you want your children to love you back, you have to be patient and caring! Not bickering, fighting, and misbehaving in front of them, overlooking their desires and wants – As I always say that children copy our behaviour!

About 8 ways of science show that Mom and Dad go wrong when they try to discipline their kids.

1. Parents fail at setting limits
2. They're overprotective and over caring
3. They nag, lecture, repeat and then yell – almost like a school teacher
4. They praise too much—and unashamedly
5. They punish too harshly and sometimes cruelly
6. They tell their child how to feel
7. They put grades and SATs ahead of creativity
8. They forget to have fun and enjoyment with their children.

❋❋

Chapter Three

From Monkeys To Humans =
Humans To Monkeys!!

Personality Is Not Set By Age: Try Schooling It It Can Change Throughout Life

When humans emerged on the face of this Earth, nobody could have believed that they are just a replica of monkeys unless Charles Darwin expounded and convinced everyone! Hence we do have some traits of a monkey in us though we might walk on this earth as human beings!

I think by now my readers have guessed the subject in question – If anytime and in any age, we do not channelize our emotions we can be as good as monkeys!

Yes we are the heirs of our ape-like ancestors, not so famous for their etiquettes and manners.

But this evolution i.e. from 'Monkey' to 'Human' was a slow and gradual process just as Darwin has pointed out.

Darwin's Theory of Evolution – Slowly But Surely...

Darwin's Theory of Evolution is a slow gradual process. Darwin wrote, "...Natural selection acts only by taking advantage of slight successive variations; she can never take a great and sudden leap, but must advance by short and sure, though slow steps.

Hence as Moulding Personalities, we have to follow Darwin's theory at any age. It all depends how much time a person takes i.e. Personality can be molded slowly and gradually at any age. 30 and after is certainly not that age where this change can't happen! All depends on your will power and inner urge!

Can We Really Change Our Personality Traits At Any Age?

Can We Really Change Our Personality Traits At Any Age?

A BEAUTIFUL, HILARIOUS AND REAL STORY TO PLEASE YOUR MIND AND WAKEN YOU FROM SLUMBER

Amod was driving with his two-year-old son Apurv, studying in kindergarten. Suddenly a rickshaw hit the sides of their newly acquired car. Apurv's father got agitated and barked an abusive at the Rickshaw Puller. Apurv really enjoyed the situation! This was his first bump with a real life hero mouthing abusive. He took immense pleasure and pride in his dad and very quickly at the same time darted his head out from the window and hurled a round of the same abusives effortlessly from his mouth and looked at his dad with great sense of pride at his glorious achievement! Amod laughed and waited to come back home to his wife.

Extremely pleased at this development, back home, his father recited this story of his son's latest acquired vocabulary to his wife very heartily. This seemed for him a moment of joy as he relished the abusive being copied and shot at the harmless man, with his unclear tongue! The wife was alarmed. She knew very well that this was the beginning of a rugged road on which now everyday her child would be journeying up and down the scale. She geared herself up and instead of paying attention to the child's latest shiny armor of defense; she started tutoring the father instead. She understood if the roots are decayed the children can never be able to acquire healthy vocabulary. Though it took some years but she eventually succeeded in schooling the Father's Traits. The Father at the age of thirty learnt his lesson!

SCHOOLING TRAITS AFTER THE AGE OF THIRTY

So we learn from the above that one can change one's personality traits at any age!

Changing your personality traits is possible at any age and it can really change your life!

"If you're ready for change, you can make it happen," says retired psychologist Jan Goldfield, PhD.

⁂⁂

Chapter Four

Change Your Personality Traits After The Age Of Thirty - Make It Possible.

A fine example in the form of story was given in the last chapter. Now here's an even more elaborate discussion on it. Until recently both professionals and laymen believed that personality traits are set by age 30. Further, psychologists believed certain personality traits are mostly genetic,

The need to change your personality type especially after 30 has arisen aggressively

which means you're born agreeable, neurotic, or extroverted – and you'll stay that way despite your environment or desire to change. You can't make any personality changes, they once believed.

But now the scenario has changed. The need to change your personality type especially after 30 has arisen aggressively and it is believed and agreed too that we can change personalities for good!

It is not only the kids and teenagers whose attributes; characteristics needs to be schooled these days. With the sudden leap of materialistic reaches, it is the generation beyond thirty which needs to be schooled more. This age group has forgotten how to behave publicly and very coolly, hide their misbehaviours in a safe cover of their 'so called DEPRESSIONS'! They try to get away with their misdeeds giving it an extenuated form of their depressed self which actually is their rude and irate behaviour.

IS IT POSSIBLE TO DEVELOP YOUR PERSONALITY AND FURTHER TO HAVE CONSTRUCTIVE REALTIONSHIP WITH YOUR CHILDREN?

Personality develops and evolves. It is in a continuous changing pattern. The way we think and behave can be molded by the indirect effect of the environment in which we dwell or the dour direct efforts made. We learn new things about the world and ourselves as we age. We are designed to be able to adapt to changes in our lives. This term is known as resiliency. Being resilient allows us to deal with change. At the same time, our personality continues to grow, change and adapt to the situations.

Who can claim very confidently that he is exactly the same person he was 5 or 10 years back? Can anyone do so? We mould ourselves according to the environment we are accidentally pushed or we chose to live!

⁂⁂

Chapter Five

PROMISES THAT PARENTS SHOULD MAKE TO THEMSELVES FOR A STRONG BONDING WITH THEIR KIDS

This is a book about schooling at the age of thirty and beyond – hence, parents' behaviour is of primary importance here.

There are two promises that every parent needs to make to become more successful.

Promise to have patience – plenty of patience. If your child is twelve years old, he has had twelve years to develop his behaviour patterns. Give your child time to change. This is where most parents fail. We have gone from one hour dry cleaning to one-hour photos to one hour eye glasses to 30 minute tune-ups. Microwave dinners, car phones and express lanes have conditioned us to expect instant gratification ion. Technology has taught us impatience. We believe that because we are trying a new idea, changes should take place overnight. Just a few days are not long enough to test a new idea. Some methods take weeks to show improvement. Be patient.

Promise to practice. Every parent must practice. Even me. My children do not care one bit that I am a teacher, who teaches parenting classes. When I'm home, I'm Mom. I get tested just like you. I have to practice, too. If you are willing to read about new ideas but do not practice them, give this book to someone else and buy a magic wand.

Children learn behaviors: Children learn good deeds and misbehavior too. Behaviour pattern is never inherited. A well-behaved child is not the result of luck. So if you misbehave, they too misbehave – If you are patient, they too will imbibe some qualities of it. Be encouraged – if children learn a particular behavioural pattern, then they can learn to change and modify it too.

Promise to have
patience – plenty of
patience

Parenting behaviour is also learned: Good parenting skills do not appear suddenly and instinctively. You can learn to be a more successful parent. But for this as I have stated earlier you have to be very patient. Your aggressive behaviour can be devastating for your child's mental and physical development.

Examine your own behaviour and determine when you are part of the problem. I want you to prepare yourself and to support yourself when your children tell you they hate you. I want you to realize and to stay calm when you are tried and tested. I want you to enable yourself to build healthy self-esteem in your children and to teach your children to think for themselves and withstand peer pressure. But the most important phenomenon is – you should know how to enjoy being a parent by schooling your behaviour.

If you want your children to be well-behaved, well-adjusted, you need to understand how your own behaviour is connected with your child's behaviour. That's what I hope to teach you in this book. I hope to teach you how to behave so your children will, too!

Changing Your Behaviour: Where to Begin

Practicing a new idea means changing your behaviour. Any change in behaviour means changing habits. Habits are not easy to change. Old habits are comfortable, new ones are not. Since it takes about a month to develop new habits, review your list two or three times a week for the next four weeks. This review will help you solidify your new habits more quickly. So in short, school your habits!

⁂⁂

Chapter Six

LESS IS MORE – TAMING YOUR MIND-TAMING POWER OF POSSESSIONS.

Simple Life – Less Worries – Channelized Behaviour – Healthy Life

Simplicity is becoming a 21st century keyword, a pursuit that is being promoted as a cure for everything from the housework blues to spiritual, social, physical, mental and economic sores.

But there is no mystery or difficulty about the concept. Simplifying our life is about gaining control over it– creating more time for our work and family to do the tasks you'd always wanted to. It's also about gaining control of mind and getting to know yourself better!

More and more people feel that they aren't spending their time on things they really enjoy or utilizing their skill set towards a job they really find satisfactory. The question that arises is – What's the point of leading a 'full life' or earning hefty figures if you don't have the time and energy to enjoy it?

Simple living is about streamlining your life and channelizing your thoughts in a way that you find time for the people and things you love. It means lightening your load, doing away with the cluttered piles you live under, as well as the debt and over-committed time required to pay for the stuff that makes up that clutter.

Everything you own costs you something, no matter how much or little you originally paid for it. Apart from the cost of acquisition, there are costs associated with a space to store your stuff, the energy to transport it, and your attention to deal with it. By having only the items that you need, you'll gain a significant cost savings by avoiding the money, space, and energy costs of clutter.

Simple living is the key to 'healthy life'. Previously we saw people overburdening their body and space with ornaments and decorative materials respectively! If they had huge space, they cluttered with woodwork but nowadays we see the same people taking out all the woodwork to create some empty space! The walls are now painted in colours emitting energy. The corners are cleared. No nonsense decoration is preferred. The floor is shining bright with ethnic, small pieces of wood material or handmade carpets finding place in their spaces! They have finally realized that less is more! If they have less things to handle, they will have more hours for themselves and their family. More things not only adds up to your work but also eats up your time which could have been utilized with your family!

If we have fewer things to handle, it will definitely add up to a healthy countenance, channelized thought process and we can take out more time for our loved ones!

How Successful Parents Behave

Have you ever seen/known any parent handling something of which they were unprepared for? Whenever I come across such a query I narrate the story of my friend Prabhat!

Prabhat's spouse became pregnant when son Parijat was almost three years old. Prabhat knew that it was vital to prepare his son for the arrival of a new baby. They wanted to avoid the dreaded effects of sibling rivalry. They read the '*New Baby*' book a dozen times. They did everything imaginable to make him feel that their new baby was also going to be his new baby. As his mom's tummy began to grow, Parijat kept a little doll tucked beneath the front of his T-shirt.

Loni's birth fascinated my friend Prabhat's son Parijat. He was so excited. Nearly everyone who brought a present for Loni, brought one for him (It was instructed by Prabhat to all visiting them). It was like Diwali in May. He loved his new sister, even though he noticed that she did not have any teeth. Everything was going just as the parents had planned.

On Loni's sixth day home, something untoward happened. Parijat hopped out of the bathtub. His rosy skin smelled like soap and baby powder. He asked his father, if he could have an apple. He said sure. Parjat reappeared a few moments later, placing one hand on the back of his father's chair while holding the apple in the other.

"Dad, I think I'm in trouble." He said.

"What for?" Prabhat asked.

"Well, when I was getting my apple, I accidentally 'peed' in the refrigerator." Parijat spoke looking very serious.

"You're right," he said. "You are in trouble."

So in the above case we see, that though the parents tried their best, the elder one developed a sense of competition with her newly born sister and tried to copy her. Maybe it was that he had this feeling that the younger one was getting more attention, which was most natural. Mothers are more with their new born.

What We Want

My children create many challenging situations. Occasionally, I am amused. Often, I feel frustrated and discouraged. Sometimes, I feel embarrassed and guilty. Our children are a measure of our success and worthiness. We judge ourselves by their success and achievements. We compare ourselves to other parents. We compare our children to other children. Have you ever watched people buy apples? We rotate each apple looking for a blemish. We hold it up to the light, examining the reflection. We squeeze each one for firmness. We study each competitor looking for the perfect apple.

We want perfect apples. Parents want successful children. We want them to be happy and well adjusted. We want them to feel good about themselves. We want children who are loving and respectful of others. We want them to be well behaved and self-motivated. We want them to be independent. All parents have the same goals and aspirations.

What We Have

Most parents confront the same behaviour problems. We become annoyed repeating everything three times. We spend too much time arguing. We become drained from the nagging and whining and manipulating and quarreling. We become exhausted from shouting and threatening. At times, it seems that all we do is punish. We feel guilty for getting angry, but it appears to be the only way to get results. We blame ourselves and feel ineffective for not knowing what to do. There are times when we dislike our children because their misbehaviour makes us feel so inadequate and miserable.

Raising well-behaved children is not easy. Many parents fail. Not because they are inadequate. Not because they lack love for their children. Not because they want something less than the best for their children. Unsuccessful parents are inconsistent. They procrastinate. They give warnings but do not follow through. They say things they do not mean. They lack patience. They punish in anger. Unsuccessful parents attend to the negative rather than the positive. They criticize too much. Parents who have discipline problems do not plan. They do not realize that they can be part of the problem. Parents are part of the problem because of their patterns of reaction.

Parents usually react in one of the two ways. Sometimes parents react passively. They give in to misbehaviour because they do not feel like confronting the problem, at least not right now. You will learn, why giving in makes misbehaviour worse. Sometimes parents react with anger. You will also learn how reacting with anger makes misbehaviour worse.

The way you react to your children's misbehaviour affects future misbehaviour. A certain amount of misbehaviour is normal. My guess is that young children misbehave about 5% of the time. (Some days it feels like 50%) Knowing how to react to this 5% is crucial. Reacting correctly and consistently can reduce misbehaviour from 5% to less than 2%. Reacting incorrectly can increase misbehavior to 10% or more.

Knowing how to react is essential. Knowing how to prevent discipline problems is more important. You

Parents who have discipline problems do not plan

can escape many predicaments by setting up a few guidelines in advance. Successful parents believe in prevention and planning. They are more proactive than reactive. You will learn several strategies to help you be more proactive.

What We Need

What factors contribute to successful parenting? Successful parents and their children are partners in discipline. Successful parents know that discipline is a teaching process. Discipline is not just punishment. Successful parents understand that their behaviour and emotions affect their children's behaviour and emotions. Successful parents model responsibility. They focus their attention and energy on the positive aspects of their children's behaviour. Successful parents emphasize cooperation, not control. Successful parents teach their children to think for themselves. They teach children self-control. Successful parents build self-esteem. They know that healthy self-esteem is the main ingredient children need to develop self-confidence and resiliency.

Successful parents learn from their children. They develop reaction patterns that reduce misbehaviour. Successful parents are consistent. They say what they mean and mean what they say. They follow through. Successful parents stay calm when their button is being pushed. They use punishments that teach, not get even. Successful parents connect special activities with good behaviour.

Successful parents anticipate problems. They have a game plan. They have proactive strategies for managing tantrums, disobedience, fighting, arguments and power struggles. Successful parents have plans that teach the value of completing chores, earning allowances, and doing homework.

Successful parents do not let misbehaviour keep them from enjoying with their children. Successful parents are strict but positive. They are serious about the importance of proper conduct, but they have a childlike sense of humour whenever it is needed. Successful parents know how to appreciate their children, even when they are misbehaving. Most importantly, successful parents are open to change.

So learn how to punish your children without feeling punished yourself. Learn how to correct your children without arguments and power struggles. Empower yourself to handle teasing and tantrums. Learn what to do when one of your children "pees" in the refrigerator. And in all these things you'll learn that it is the 'patience' factor which eventually helps you. Patience here does not mean that you have to handle problems by giving undue liberty and spoiling the child – patience means handling situations, making your own pattern of techniques.

If you already have well-behaved children, thank your higher power. This book will help you too. It will make you more conscious of the successful strategies you are currently using. This book will help you maintain good behaviour and prepare you for any future problems.

One of the best sources of help for parents is other parents. Parenting Workshops can be a boon. Here parents share their ideas and help each other by quoting their experiences and how they eventually 'tamed' their children without facing 'the guilt problem'.

I have tried to put across what I have gathered from different parents. Parents who were fatigued and confused. Parents drained from yelling. Parents who felt imprisoned by their children. Parents who walked through life on a treadmill. Parents whose hearts were empty. Parents who sometimes felt like giving up. Parents who discovered a better way.

All the examples in this book are true stories from actual parents with real problems. The ideas discussed are simple and practical. Everything is explained in the bread and butter style of writing (often associated with Pablo Neruda), simple yet elegant. There are a number of theories about parent and child behaviour. Most authors accept one theory. They try to convince you that their ideas work for every parent and every child. After trying this approach, I decided it was insufficient.

Since every parent and child is unique, why not use a variety of methods? Use the best from every theory. Not all of them will work all the time. You need to select the ideas that make sense to you.

How We Learn Parenting Behaviour

We acquired most of our Parenting behaviour from our parents. Have you ever said something to your children and then realized you heard these same words when you were a child. "Be careful or you'll break your neck." "Be quiet and eat." We parent the way we were parented. We discipline as we were disciplined. Most ideas that we learned from our parents are helpful. Some are not. We pick and choose from these methods. Things we like, we use. Things we do not like, we do not use.

We also learn by watching other parents for good ideas. We learn by talking with friends. We learn from their experiences. They learn from our experiences. We share techniques that work.

We also learn by trial and error. Much of what we do with our children is based on our best guess at the time. Some things work; some fail. This happens to us all. Every first-born child is a test for most parents. You begin using trial and error the moment you get home from the hospital. I remember feeling confused and helpless. The baby is crying. What does it mean? Hungry? Lonely? Wet? Too warm? Too cold? Trial and error also applies to discipline. If sending your child to bed early works once, you will probably use it again.

The beliefs that you already have about parenting and discipline are fine. Learning from your parents and friends and learning by trial and error is normal. Add judgment and common sense and you have the substance for a solid foundation. This book will build on that foundation.

Love Does Not Always Light the Way

Too many parents have the false belief that if they love their children as much as possible, misbehaviour will someday improve. Love, warmth and affection are essential. They are fundamental. You also need knowledge.

Imagine you needed an operation. As you were about to be put under the anesthetic, your physician whispers in your ear. "I want you to know that I am not a surgeon. I'm not a doctor at all. Please don't worry. My parents are both doctors. I have a lot of friends who are doctors. I've asked a lot of questions about surgery. Just relax! I have a lot of common sense and I love my patients very much." Would you let this person use a scalpel on you?

Parents need training just as professionals need training. Children need trained parents as much as they need loving parents. Training pulls together all the good ideas you already have. Training provides structure and direction. Training provides a framework. Training gives you confidence. You learn what you are doing is right. More confidence means more self-control, less anger, less guilt and less frustration. More confidence means more respect from your children. Without confidence, many parents are afraid to correct or punish their children. Some worry that their children will not like them. Some are afraid they might harm their children emotionally. So they let their children misbehave.

It Wasn't Like That When I Was Growing Up

Why doesn't discipline work the way it did 20 or 30 years ago? Why don't the old-fashioned methods work? Why is being a parent so demanding and confusing? Parenting is more difficult because childhood is more difficult. Children are under pressure. Pressure to make adult decisions with the experience and emotions of a child. Pressure from peers. Pressure from school. Pressure from the media. Pressure that seeps down from the pressures on the parents. Pressure on our children translates into problems for us.

There are several changes in our culture that have a tremendous impact on discipline and our roles as parents. Our economy has created financial tension in families. Parents come home stressed. Their fuse is short. The rising divorce rate affects all of our children. Today, there are schools where 4 out of 5 children have experienced divorce. Single parenting is stressful.

Twenty years ago, everyone in the same town or neighborhood had the same values and beliefs. No matter where you went to play, the rules were the same. Everyone's parents had the same expectations. This is no longer true. Every family has their own standards. Our children experience many versions of right and wrong. This is confusing to children.

How do these changes in our society affect the way you discipline your children? Why won't the old ways work today? The old ways were simple solutions for a society with simple problems. Today's problems are more complicated. They require refined solutions. Our children live in the future, not the past. We have to cope with the adversity of our times. If you want to be a successful parent, you have to know how to discipline today's children. Parents need training. Not because parents are incapable, but because parenting is no longer simple.

⁂⁂

Chapter Seven

Sibling Rivalry: Thirty And Beyond

SHOULDN'T 'THIS' BE SCHOOLED BEFORE THE DAMAGE IS DONE?

According to Wikipedia:

Sibling rivalry describes the competitive relationship or animosity between siblings, blood-related or not. Often competition is the result of a desire for greater attention from parents. However, even the most conscientious parents can expect to see sibling rivalry in play to a degree.

Often competition is the result of a desire for greater attention from parents

Children tend to naturally compete with each other for not only attention from parents but for recognition in the world.

"Siblings generally spend more time together during childhood than they do with parents. The sibling bond is often complicated and is influenced by factors such as parental treatment, birth order, personality, and people and experiences outside the family.

According to Child Psychologists, Sibling Rivalry is particularly intense when children are very close in age and of the same gender, or where one child is intellectually gifted than the other.

There is an Arabic saying:

"Me against my brother; my brother and me against my cousin; me, my brother, and my cousin against the stranger…."

Sibling rivalry can involve aggression; however, it is not the same as sibling abuse where one child victimizes another.

Adult Sibling Rivalry (A web help)

Sibling rivalry often lingers through adulthood.

The new view holds that conflict is not the natural state of sibling relationships. Still, for a third of us, discord sown early endures for a lifetime.

Karuna Kailash made a new commitment: "I'm going to keep the communication open between my sister and me," the 44-year-old media consultant told. "I will follow the rules... do whatever it takes to make our relationship work. You can bet on it!"

That Karuna's younger sister (an identical twin whose twin died within days of their premature birth) and Karuna had never gotten along didn't seem to matter. Karuna was willing to forget about the seven beloved pet golden butterflies, her sister had let out of the window, one at a time. She was ready to look beyond her sister's angry reminders. And she was able, she thought, to forgive her sister for turning their adult years into one explosion after another.

That was three years ago. Today Karuna has given up, finding herself at a "total loss as to how to smooth things out." At home in Ahmedabad for her father's funeral last spring, Karuna, her sister, her brother, and her mother (divorced from their father years before) spent some time together. "I ceased to exist," Karuna said. "I became wallpaper. No one talked to me. And, for once, I didn't feel any pain. It was like, 'Ah, so this is how it was with us.' I saw things the way they were and are, not the way I wished they were or could have been. Not long after, I resolved not to have anything to do with my sister or the rest of the family. I don't want it!"

While few adult siblings have severed their ties completely, approximately one-third of them describe their relationship as cold or distant. They don't get along with their sibling or have little in common, spend limited time together, and use words like "competitive," "humiliating," and "hurtful" to depict their childhoods.

The speed with which old conflicts reduce these adults to children again, prevents them from seeing one another in a new or different light.

They push each other's buttons without knowing why or how and recast themselves in childhood roles that never worked in the first place.

When they talk about their brothers and sisters, adult siblings locked into old patterns resort to a variety of emotional strategies. Some try to diminish the relationship (and their feelings) by emphasizing the importance of friends and spouses instead.

Some speak with frightening venom as they describe the horrors of growing up under the same roof. Others become very analytical, piecing together all

Sibling rivalry began with the story of Cain and Abel

that went wrong between them, thereby detailing the impossibility of ever finding a common ground. For most conflicted brothers and sisters, there is an underlying sense that "this is the way it's supposed to be."

Western culture has an obsession with sibling rivalry that began with the story of Cain and Abel and was elaborated by Freud, who labeled and dwelt on the competition between siblings for parental love and attention. It's coloured our perception of sibship ever since. Therapists and laymen alike tend to view the relationship largely as one of struggle and controversy. We have no rituals that make, break, or celebrate the sibling bond. And family experts have underemphasized the sibling relationship, instead concentrating on parents and children and husbands and wives. Some wonder that sibling rivalry is accepted as the normal state of affairs.

From Genes to Scenes

There is a consensus among clinicians and developmental psychologists that the sibling bond is complicated, fluid, and influenced by many factors. Parental treatment, genetics, gender, life events, ethnic and generational patterns, and people and experiences outside the family all contribute to the success or failure of a particular sibling connection. To understand how these factors shape the lives of siblings, researchers have begun looking at young siblings within the context of their immediate families.

I have read that at the forefront of this work is a famous Psychologist whose pioneering sibling studies are being conducted in her native England and in the United States.

Through her observational studies of siblings at home instead of in the lab, her work presents a radically revised view of children's abilities and their social understanding. She now knows that from the startlingly young age of one year, siblings respond to disputes between their siblings by supporting or punishing one of the antagonists. These same young siblings are profoundly affected by their mother's interaction with the other siblings.

"The message is," the Psychologist said, "that children are far more socially sophisticated than we ever imagined. That little 15-month-old or 17-month-old is watching like a hawk what goes on between her mother and older sibling. And the greater the difference in the maternal affection and attention, the more hostility and conflict between the siblings." From 18 months on siblings understand how to comfort, hurt, and exacerbate each other's pain. They understand family rules, can differentiate between transgressions of different sorts, and can anticipate the response of adults to their own and to other people's misdeeds.

By age three, children have a sophisticated grasp of how to use social rules for their own ends. They can evaluate themselves in relation to their siblings and possess the developmental skills necessary to adapt to frustrating circumstances and relationships in the family. Whether they have the drive to adapt, to get along with a sibling whose goals and interests may be different from their own, can make the difference between a cooperative or rivalrous relationship, Dunn insists.

Now readers, don't you think that there is a need to channelize the feelings and ways of the elders who feel trapped in such kind of emotions? Shouldn't be there some kind of school to train the constant mongers mentally so that they do not suffer from feelings of repentance in their later years? Don't you think their misdeeds sprouting out of their jealousies and unhealthy competition be channelized within time so that they do not suffer from a feeling of guilt?

The above and many other such examples stress on the need of some grooming school for these 'middle aged mongers'! And the sooner the better. In a way these people will not only save their lives, their relationships but also redeem the society. In fact their careless attitude sometimes becomes a pain in the neck. Remember when you were small, you were being taught by your parents to be soft and well-behaved. At that point of time perhaps you too might have felt that your parents are trying to teach you etiquettes which they themselves lack ... We should realize that before taming our children, we should tame ourselves. Today's time and scenario is quite different – youngsters will definitely retaliate unlike that of the golden old times. The generation has changed and so has the mentality. Today, the youngsters immediately reply back and enter into an altercation with their elders. So it is better to save your self-esteem and guide your children by wearing the right kind of attitude at the right time and doing away with callous and irresponsible attitudes.

A FAMOUS INDIAN SIBLING RIVALRY STORY: THE AMBANI BROTHERS' BRICKBATTING!

This comes right from a saas-bahu type serial when the patriarch of a rich family passes away leaving a fortune behind to his two able sons, hoping they would spread his legacy far and beyond. I'm not sure whether Mr Dhirubhai Ambani would have liked the way his legacy – Reliance Industries has split up.

Ever since Ambani senior died, his sons Mukesh and Anil Ambani have sliced and diced his company and created their own version of their father's empire, but the buck does not stop there, the rivalry has taken a turn for the worse with their battles often taking a legal course.

REASONS OF SIBLING RIVALRY

Why you may resent your sibling?

"I can't stop resenting her! She was always the 'bright one', the 'gifted one', it was obvious that my parents considered her the 'pretty one'. I love her, but when I see her now, I just feel this horrible envy – even after all these years!"

Sibling rivalry can cast its shadow for a lifetime. One of my colleagues had a very destructive relationship with her sister. I was reminded uncomfortably of the 1962 movie '*WHATEVER HAPPENED TO BABY JANE*", in which two aging sisters, Blanche and Jane live together in mutual enmity and hate. Let us get to the heart of the story:

At one point in this movie, knowing that she is near death, Blanche tells Jane the truth about what happened years before. It was she, Blanche, who had tried to run over her once drunken sister. Jane, however, had moved out of the way in time and Blanche had slammed into the gate and snapped her own spine, managing to drag herself out of the car. Because Jane was too drunk to realize what happened she has since believed that she was responsible for her sister's condition. Jane pathetically asks, "You mean all this time we could have been friends?" With her mental condition completely deteriorated, Jane runs off to a beach-side concession booth to get ice-cream cones for the two of them. The police arrive to find Jane as she dances on the sand, with a crowd surrounding her. Finally she again has the attention that she's craved, and she dances, joyfully, happy at last in her decayed imagination. The police spot a motionless Blanche lying on the sand and hurry over to help her as the film ends. Whether Blanche has survived is not revealed!

SO we see that the sisters wasted so many years of their precious lives. Moreover in a bid to take avenge and jealous of Jane's fame, Blanche ruined her own life!

Sibling rivalry: Loving and hating

All siblings compete to some extent and ideally, feelings of unfairness drop away with the years. But chronic sibling rivalry can be complex. You might love your sibling but resent them. What's more, the intensity of your resentment can leave you baffled: "I'm an adult now; why does it still hurt so much?" Loving someone and resenting them can be hard.

Sometimes it's easier and simpler, though of course not better, just to hate someone.

Rivalry happens when sibling competition becomes:

Almost constant

Damaging to self-esteem and confidence

Damaging to the relationship with the sibling

Ongoing through the years

Damaging to the relationship with the parents

So for what, exactly, do siblings compete?

1. Attention: A scarce resource

We all need attention. Think of it as a food. Some of us are pretty good at getting just enough attention – and some of us feel we need a constant supply. (Ever noticed how fading celebrities accustomed to constant attention may seek increasingly desperate ways to cling onto it? If you pay little attention, you'll see how many of our Bollywood stars behave abnormally when any new comer is on the block or if they are ageing!

The point is, attention from parents is a scarce resource. You can't have all of it all the time. It needs to be shared out, and you must understand this. By cribbing that the other one is getting more attention than you and ruining your mental health as well as your overall personality and relationships, you are bound to take it out on those who interact with you.

Ever seen young chicks competing with their siblings for food – desperate and open-mouthed? Rival siblings compete, just as fervently, for the attention of their parents.

If you feel that your parents give more of the available praise, encouragement, concern, and high regard to your brother or sister than to you, you may feel cheated. It will feel unfair! It's not surprising that feelings of resentment become directed toward the sibling.

So why would parents give one child more attention than another? Here I feel parents, more than the children, require some kind of school to do away with their biased behaviour. This callous behaviour is responsible for sowing seeds of rivalry among siblings. Parents often praise the gifted one in front of the repressed one and here is where the animosity between siblings starts brewing. Every child is not the same and the parents have to be schooled about it so that they abstain from their irresponsible behaviour! Let us read actually what this means.

The 'special child': FAVOURING ONE CHILD OVER OTHER!

Parents may inadvertently (and unconsciously) favour one child over another for all kinds of different reasons. Maybe that child was the first born, or last born, or proves to be good at something the parents always dreamed they'd be good at themselves. I remember one mother say that her youngest daughter had the musical talent of which she, herself, had always dreamed. Parents can assign roles to their children:

"Rita is the understanding one."

"Shalu is the intelligent one."

"Seetu is the problem creator."

The 'special child' may have behavioural problems or even be ill. They may use bad behaviour as a way of 'cheating' extra attention out of their parents. Or because they are ill or have extra special needs through some condition, they may simply and inevitably require more attention. The sibling may resent them for this and feel guilty for this resentment.

2. *Role play: Concocted by others!*

When other people concoct roles for us, we can quite easily come to play out these roles. We can, of course, also rebel – often in adolescence. Roles we 'play' in childhood can determine our behaviour for decades – especially in relation to our families. And the fact remains that years later we may still find ourselves saying stuff like: "You were always the clever/sensible/pretty one!"

A real story of my friend Preeti and her sister Suman (names changed):

My friend Preeti was very beautiful. When she was sixteen, she was the favourite of all her teachers and she bagged all the roles of beautiful heroines to be enacted in school dramas. Her sister Suman was seven years younger to her. Though pretty but nowhere in comparison to her sister Preeti. Suman was however academically strong and serious but their parents too were over protective of Preeti as they considered her to be 'the beautiful one'! So Preeti had developed a habit of absorbing all the limelight. No one paid attention to Suman….

Tables had after some time turned as Suman was very talented and intelligent. The once gawky girl was hailed and appreciated by everyone. Preeti could not digest this. Though she loved her sister but in a bid to look more attractive than her sister, her visit to beauty parlours increased manifold – the result – her skin had aged in her early thirties itself! And it was here where the actual strife started. Preeti would not leave a single chance to demean her sister Suman publicly. She could not tolerate the 'beauty and personality of her younger sister Suman, which made her gain all the attention instead of her. Suman in fact ignored everything and tried to patch up with her sister but Preeti's self-centeredness made her extremely selfish. She even tried to create misunderstandings between Suman and her husband by spreading false stories about Suman and her alleged link ups! A stage reached where Preeti though married tried to woo her own sister's husband younger to her by about three years! Now here where Suman decided to segregate all relationships with her sister!

Almost about a decade has passed; the sisters are no longer in talking terms. Suman's heart sometimes grieves and she wants to patch up but now Suman's children admonish and stop her from maintaining any kind of relationship which grieves her all the more. They do not want their middle-aged mother to face any problem in the age that she is now.

Now whenever I hear any gossip circulating about these sisters in our friend circle, I simply feel that there should have been some kind of school to make them understand and realize the end purpose of their lives. A day will come when both will become very old and probably then they'll realize that their fight was frivolous and had no meaning!

Another Side of Sibling Rivalry

Siblings can resent the fact that – what is expected and 'allowed' for their sibling isn't for them. A man told me that he felt that his parents quite admired his brother for travelling the world and "doing exactly as he wanted", whereas whenever he tried to go his own way, they would frown upon it.

So how does this 'Sibling Rivalry' shape up as they age?

Sibling rivalry and regression

Situations can make us regress. Middle-aged men might enter the situation of an old school reunion and find themselves feeling, even acting, in ways they had thirty years before. Even elderly siblings can 'revert to type' when they meet up and regress to feelings they had fifty years before.

"Every time I see her, I feel uncertain, dowdy, incompetent, and jealous; but I never usually feel like that!"

Nature has its own needs

Another important step is to constantly remember that you can only be you. I'm often struck by the fact how different siblings are to one another.

Brothers and sisters can sometimes seem quite opposite in their characters. It's thought that about 50% of how we behave is genetically determined. It also seems that nature needs all kinds of different types of people to populate the planet.

Do away with comparison

Not all bees can, or should, be queens – there have to be accountants, nurses and other bees too. I think now you have got my point. Nature needs to scatter different types of people into the world because different types of people are needed. Perhaps you are supposed to be very different from your sibling. So parents and teachers as well as others should understand that all people cannot be same and this planet moreover cannot be run if all people were like each other. We need different people with different skills to constitute a society/state or in whole this Earth!

Eventually, we need to disentangle our sense of identity from the conditioning and expectations placed upon us when we were very young.

Who do you want to be?

It is not that when you were small, your parents wanted you to be an Engineer or a Doctor, just like your elder siblings, you have to become one! You should have the acumen and determination to determine your path and life. Parents have full right to guide you but when you are not able to cope up with certain situations, you have to speak to them and let them know your mind! They might seem stubborn at times and may not relent. In such situations, you can take help of school/college Counsellors.

You are not your brother or sister. But it is very important that you can begin to relate to them as other adults without resentment or bitterness. If there is resentment or bitterness, naturally rivalry will brew up!

⁕⁕

Chapter Eight

MONEY AND SELF-CONTENTMENT

It Is Not Only the Men – Women too forget Manners!

We are going to discuss here that it is not only men who generally behave obnoxiously to get what they want in life. It is also the woman who forgets her manners and self-esteem. Especially when it comes to money matters!

In fact in a race to achieve the best of all lives, sometimes they lose their very important relationships. Their manners and behaviour becomes obnoxious. The cut-throat competitive world leads them almost to the brink of extinction. Actually in a quest to achieve more for their families and dear ones, they in fact forget that somewhere they are losing their valuable and precious relationships – The same children, for whom they are working hard, are drifting away from them emotionally. Money is important, but there is never an end to any need. If you have one pair of shoes, you want two – If you have two, you want three. The greed is non-ending. SO AT THE END OF THE DAY SELF-CONTENTMENT IS MORE IMPORTANT!

Moving ahead with life I have realized, there are always some days of exile in everyone's life – Some admit/some don't and some are perhaps very lucky not to have them at all!

In my days of exile and gloominess I fought back with quite a meditative fervor – I read and read and made books my companion and best friend – I wrote and made my expressions my pillar of support to sustain life...AND I WON: I SPRUNG BACK ON THE SPRINGBOARD OF LIFE – NOW LIFE SOMETIMES ASKS ME "TELL ME HOW YOU DID IT?" MY ANSWER: I JUST MOVED AWAY WITH TIME TRYING TO CATCH ITS FLOW. This is not self-conceitedness; this is just a feeling I wanted to share.

I did not crib and cry. I did not feel jealous of others.

Yes, I cannot deny that the 'obvious thought' was there – 'Why me?' But there is no answer to this question. Why life pulls you down and bestows others with luck has no answer. I also, instead of wasting my time, getting aggressive and blaming others paved a creative path for myself. I realized, that time never waits for anyone and I have to make the most of it. Sometimes I was laughed upon as many felt I was just wasting my time in going ahead with my studies. Sometimes, I was purposely disparaged and insulted so that I lose my energy to achieve what I want. And it is not that I didn't feel a 'setback' or 'felt frustrated', I felt like ending my life too but never became outrageous.

But ending one's life is also not any solution. No one is there to cry after you are gone. For few days people remember you but the need to sustain and existence overpowers the emotions of those who were once so near to you and almost dependent on you. Hence I realized, Life is to be lived – in any case it is to be lived. So why not make it meaningful. Believe it or not, there are forces in this world which help you if you are determined. I had not only been mentally quashed but was physically harmed too. But now what is the end result. I am here writing for you all to come back in the main stream of life with a determination that never was.

But the thirst to gain knowledge didn't dry out in my heart – It became a perennial quest. And I succeeded.

And now I want to share a similar story of one of my students (name changed).

ANUMEHA'S STORY
: A WOMAN'S STORY AND REVELATION
: CONSEQUENCES OF YESTERYEARS EXPERIENCE ON RELATIONSHIPS

Anumeha's story:

"I" here is Anumeha

A newly found friend said to me, 'Has something happened to you in the past?'

I avoided this question for months until I felt safe enough to say what had been happening.

I told him how I have grown up seeing my parents fight and how I went and slept with every second guy, just to seek mental and emotional support. How I became addicted to drugs as I just wanted to forget everything happening in my life. I believed nothing good was happening. This continued for years. My personality would have remained the same and I might have never

been able to come out of the trap unless a friend of mine supported me to seek help.

It was the hardest but best thing that I could have done. To talk and read about people going through the same troubles was a great help for me. To know I was not alone anymore and realising that it wasn't my fault was a good feeling.

I'm now 35 and I am working in a women's refuge for domestic violence. Post the age of thirty I would have remained the same, if my friend wouldn't have helped me. Now, I work with the children who come in to the refuge. It's a rewarding job, being able to assist the children in living with and leaving domestic violence.

I love life – I have a gorgeous husband and son with another baby on the way.

I believe if I could come out of my cocoon of unhappiness and depression to achieve my goals and could mould my mind to believe that life really is a good thing, then it is possible for other young comrades of my age too.

I can learn to re-establish that a person can trust someone. Never let that trust be broken.

I can learn to agree and disagree in an appropriate manner.

I can learn that it's OK to be happy, sad and all the in-between.

I can learn to win, lose and enjoy the game.

Life is not always a game. It can hurt.

I know I need nurturing, comforting, caring, hugging. I need to have healthy role models with all the human characteristics and attributes. We all need these things.

What does it mean to care? I can speak words to care. I can give someone time when I care. I can give someone gifts when I care. I can do things for them when I care. I can feel my senses when I care.

> I can hear words when someone cares for me. I can be given time when they care. I can receive gifts when they care. They do things for me when they care. They have feelings when they care….

So we see Anumeha suffered. People can suffer in any age. This sufferance can alter their mannerisms and behaviour in a negative way. They can become depressed, rowdy, careless and negligent about themselves and people around them.

⁂⁂

Chapter Nine

THIRTY AND 'BLAME GAME'

In 'Work-Family Conflict': Learn accepting Your Share of Fame/Defame.

A new study by Elizabeth M. Poposki, Ph.D., assistant professor of psychology in the School of Science at Indiana University-Purdue University Indianapolis, explores day-to-day experiences in attributing this type of blame. The work examines individual incidents of work-family conflict and tracks how blame for this conflict is attributed.

Only three percent of those surveyed blamed both work and family for conflict between the two. Sixty-four percent of those surveyed blamed work, not family, for conflict. Twenty-two percent blamed only their family role. Five percent blamed external factors other than work or family for the conflict, and only six percent blamed themselves for the conflict. There were no gender differences in how blame was assigned.

These individuals mostly above thirty and beyond attributed conflict to external sources rather than blaming the conflict on themselves and hence were more likely to experience anger and frustration following the conflict.

The following “tasks of life” were introduced by Venerable Master Hsing Yun, the founder of Fo Guang Shan Monastery in 2005. They can be regarded as our motto for life –

Between Self and Others

1. When you help others, you are also helping yourself. Your consideration towards others also means care and love for yourself.

2. Cater to those who wish to do good, and recognize a common goal with them.. Oblige others and respect their wishes in order for a bright future to exist.

3. Be modest and courteous in associating with the world. Be humble and willing to learn, make necessary concessions to accommodate the general situation, and be understanding toward others.

4. Be gentle and humble when dealing with others. Show kindness through speech and facial expressions to make others feel as if they are bathing in the spring breeze.

5. Harmony, calmness and peace are the keys to interpersonal harmony. Diligence, hard-work and assiduity are the keys to success.

6. Treat others with honesty and strive to achieve satisfaction for all. Treat your guests with respect to make them feel at home.

7. When you meet other people, say at least three sentences to them, and accompany them for a round. Be reasonable at all times and always put a smile on your face.

8. Respect, praise, and tolerance are a triad for keeping good relations with the world.

9. Refrain from verbosity in times of joy, and do not take your anger out on others.

10. Listen well, and take note of the essence of what others have to say.

11. Never hit the nail directly on the head; learn the noble art of subtlety.

12. Reproach someone with comforting words, criticize with compliments, reprimand with praises, and give orders with respect.

13. Be sincere, passionate, and polite. Utilize the following words often in your speech: “please”, “thank you” and “sorry”.

14. Educate and praise youngsters; care for and look after the elderly; guide and assist the disable; advise and be considerate towards the depressed.

15. Care for your neighbours and community, and participate in local events. Help and keep guard for each other, and coexist in harmony.

16. Attend to your parents and seniors, and be filial to them. Give younger ones opportunities, and offer guidance whenever needed.

17. Frequently help others without asking for anything in return. Do good whenever possible, and be a virtuous and delightful volunteer worker for the human world.

18. Listen to the words of kindness and never forget their meaning. One must not become a "nonhuman".

19. Always be responsible, for reason is fair, upright and equal for all.

20. Retain the ability for self-reflection under all circumstances. Never blame everyone and everything else for your unhappiness, for every matter has its own cause and effect.

21. Do not be jealous of those who have done good deeds, spoken kind words or are respected by others. Instead, be determined to follow their examples.

22. Be thankful to the kindhearted, be grateful to the helpful, and be touched by acts of virtue.

23. Frequently do something which touches people's hearts, and also allow yourself to be touched by the kindness of others.

24. Learn to accept disadvantages, false accusations, setbacks, and humiliation, and then you will be ready to accept glory.

25. Subject yourself to ascetic trainings to strengthen yourself in life, even ten years of it is not too much.

26. Set your mind on one to three lifetime role models and resolve to follow their examples.

27. It is necessary to be friends with virtuous ones in life. When you encounter virtuous teachers, be sure to stay close to them, be loyal and never disobey them.

28. Relinquish unreasonable attachment, and accept the truth with a humble mind. Only humility brings good, while arrogance causes nothing but unfavourable outcomes.

29. Discover your greatest shortcoming, be willing to correct it, and put your vow into thorough practice.

30. The ability to admit your faults is the greatest virtue. It is also the greatest courage of all.

31. Remember what wrong you have done, constantly remind yourself of it, and never make the same mistake again.

32. Self-reflect before you blame others for their mistakes, for only a fair assessment of your merits and faults gives you the right to judge others.

33. Cherish life, care for life, respect life and never hurt life.

34. Do not be blinded by love; do not betray yourself for money.

35. Learn to accept disadvantages and even teach yourself that they are actually advantages.

36. Meditate for at least five minutes or read a prayer from Beads of Pearl: Prayers for Engaged Living every day.

37. Spend at least half a day in solitude once a week for self-reflection. Be a vegetarian at least one day every month to nurture your heart of compassion.

38. Practice the three acts of goodness everyday: do good things, say good words, and think good thoughts.

39. Observe the Seven Virtues in your daily life: no drugs, no pornography, no violence, no

stealing, no gambling, no alcohol, and no harsh speech.

40. Have deep faith in the Dharma and constantly contemplate all virtues. Refrain from doing anything unwholesome, and practice all good.

41. Always keep the promise you have made, because a promise cannot be taken back once it is made.

42. Feel shame for what you do not know, what you are incapable of, what makes you impure, and what makes you unkind, for shame is like a garland that adorns us.

43. Think of what is good and beautiful instead of what is sad and sorrowful. Turn your mind into a factory that produces nothing but good.

44. Always have sympathy and pray for unfortunate ones no matter where you are.

45. The ability to give brings true wealth; the ability to give brings true gain.

46. Cultivate merits by giving according to what your ability, role, willingness, and conditions allow.

47. Organ donation helps prolong life and also offers a new life to waste-material.

48. Develop the capacity to treat others by the following concepts: you are important while I am not, you have while I don't, you are happy while I suffer, you are right while I am wrong.

49. Do not be suspicious or jealous of others. Merit comes from helping others fulfill their goals as well as treating others with kindness.

50. Do not cling to gains and losses; do not compare with others what you have or have not.

51. Never infect others with your own sadness, and never bring your worries to bed.

52. Learn to improve your mind, reform your character, turn around, and make necessary U-turn in life.

53. Be consistent in your behaviour and understanding. Do not be enlightened in theory but ignorant in practice.

IS IT DIFFICULT TO PRACTICE AND EASY TO PREACH?

YES IT IS!!

I have often seen that we get angry over petty issues but when it comes to others, we start preaching.

Preaching and teaching is easy but following the same thing is difficult.

The above points are suggestions for you as well as for me. Being a human, I too have the vile instincts and attitudes hidden in me. These instincts are sometimes hidden and curbed. But at times, these can surface and drown me. So if we/you seriously follow some of the above mentioned points – we can reprimand the animal in us and rise on the platform of humanity!

❋❋

Chapter Ten

Thirty Plus and Jealousy

Human Interest In Darker Side Is Timeless

Though we have gone through many points to correct ourselves but there are still some zones left to consider. Let us have a look at the lines below and try to understand what they say.

"You shall not covet your neighbour's house; you shall not covet your neighbour's wife, or his male servant, or his female servant, or his ox, or his donkey, or anything that is your neighbour's." Exodus.

The deadly sins of human nature – arrogance, jealousy, envy, ego, snobbishness, stubbornness, etc increases as we grow up. On one side the grownups ask their children not to be vile, selfish and aggressive, on the other hand, they themselves indulge in such games!

Almost nobody would say, "I'm envious that you're better-looking than I am." You can't change the way you or the other person looks. Few people would admit, "I'm envious that you have a spouse and children while I haven't had a relationship in years." To admit to such feelings acknowledges a level of hatred most personal relationships can't tolerate. For the truth is that envy, the green-eyed monster, wants to destroy what it cannot have. The "solution" to envy — the way to find relief from the suffering it causes if you can't have what you envy for yourself — is to destroying it. Aesop's fable about the fox and the grapes speaks of unbearable desire but also describes a psychic mechanism (spoiling) active when envy comes into place.

Driven by hunger, a fox tried to reach some grapes hanging high on the vine but was unable to, although he leaped with all his strength. As he went away, the fox remarked, 'Oh, you aren't even ripe yet! I don't need any sour grapes.' People who speak disparagingly of things that they cannot attain would do well to apply this story to themselves.

In her version of Jean De La Fontaine's the most famous French fabulist, retelling of the fable, Marianne Moore underlines his ironical comment on the situation in a final pun, "Better, I think, than an embittered whine" makes the envied object less worthy of that. That is the less the fox thinks of the grapes, the more happy he will be – and more so if he thinks that the grapes were not at all fit to be eaten.

Although the fable describes purely subjective behaviour, the English idiom, 'sour grapes', which develops from the story, is now often used also of envious disparagement to others. Similar expressions exist in other language and there is a similar idiom in the Scandavian Countries but there the fox makes its comment about rowanberries since grapes are not common in northern latitudes.

Socrce: http://en.wikipedia.org/wiki/
The_Fox_and_the_Grapes

In India we have the same story in Hindi. '*Angoor Khatte Hai*'. Here too, we see that the fox wants to get the enticing grapes alluring one of the branches of a vine and when he couldn't have, he simply pulls a long face and makes them unworthy of his personality by belittling and disparaging their worth.

Maybe he did the right thing to divert his mind from a particular thing which he couldn't have. But actually sometimes people do not understand this. Their anxiety to achieve a certain thing in life becomes their passion and from passion changes into obsession. And when it becomes obsession then it becomes a disease. Passion is advocated to the extent it fosters your mental growth but from the point where passion becomes more prominent than your original personality, is dangerous. It thus has shades of violent jealousy which finally dooms the lives of those burning in its flames.

Passion in teenagers is quite common but then too I would not advocate to the 'Killer Extent'. But Passion leading to obsession becomes KILLER in people above the age of thirty, as they without realizing reach out and race for things just to show down their competitors. Healthy competition is always advocated but a competition which becomes passion and culminates into obsession is a BIG NO.

⁂⁂

Chapter Eleven

Facebook And Relationships

Jealousy Thy Name Is Human

These days Facebook is playing a very important role in our lives. To say that it is an added headache for the Parents would be definitely wrong as Facebook is not only confined to the youngsters but the older ones too are in its grip.

I realize that I, too got in touch with my first Publisher through Facebook. There was a long discussion.

Then emails were exchanged. Finally my first book was launched.

But undoubtedly this is also a crude truth that Facebook is creating a lot of virtual relationships and friends. And in all this it creates jealousy/ rivalry and other menial and negative attitudes. And if it was amongst the teenagers, one would have been a little less worried but interestingly 'Facebook' has taken people of all ages in its grip – especially those who are in their thirties or above. The problem hence starts here. The people in this age group are expected to guide their children and youngsters and not fight over 'petty statuses'. So you see tension at the workplace, and tension/ jealousy/rivalry in the virtual world too where you venture for relaxation!

According to Discovery News:

"After a stressful day fighting the battles of the real world, you sit down at your computer for a virtual vacation with only one destination in mind: Facebook. The familiarity of your friends' smiling faces in conjunction with the simple blue and white design begin to wash away the troubles of the day until your newsfeed reports a disturbing development.

Your boyfriend's unjustly attractive ex-girlfriend has just written a comment on his wall, expressing her

Facebook is creating jealousy/ rivalry and other menial and negative attitudes

gratitude for the time they spent together last week. You blink ferociously, your shirt clings to your skin as you begin to sweat and your virtual vacation turns into an information-induced, Internet inferno.

As if being in a relationship weren't difficult enough, human sexuality researcher and PhD candidate at the University of Guelph in Canada, Amy Muise, explained how Facebook can further contribute to relationship".

According to Amy Muise:

"The social network site Facebook is a rapidly expanding phenomenon that is changing the nature of social relationships. Anecdotal evidence, including information described in the popular media, suggests that Facebook may be responsible for creating jealousy and suspicion in romantic relationships. The objectives of the present study were to explore the role of Facebook in the experience of jealousy and to determine if increased Facebook exposure predicts jealousy above and beyond personal and relationship factors. Three hundred eight undergraduate students completed an online survey that assessed demographic and personality factors and explored respondents' Facebook use. A hierarchical multiple regression analysis, controlling for individual, personality, and relationship factors, revealed that increased Facebook use significantly predicts Facebook-related jealousy. We argue that this effect may be the result of a feedback loop whereby using Facebook exposes people to often ambiguous information about their partner that they may not otherwise have access to and that this new information incites further Facebook use. Our study provides evidence of Facebook's unique contributions to the experience of jealousy in romantic relationships.

Well, let's focus on the one thing that is quite popular these days: Facebook. One of my friends in her last relationship, became jealous at every single comment or 'like' made on the page of her boyfriend by a female. Even if she was married or was decades older than him. She just felt terribly jealous. But gradually she has learned to control this, but it's something that did not in any way help her relationship.

As Quoted by Discovery News:

Amy Muise's take on jealousy

How Facebook Breeds Jealousy

The more time people spend on the social networking site, the more jealous they get.

1. It's Addictive

Curse that Mark Zuckerberg for creating this online crack! No matter how you try to fight it, Facebook keeps calling you back… and that's the problem.

The more time people spent on Facebook the more jealous they were. Even after Muise's experiment controlled for factors of trust, self-esteem, and relationship commitment, "… time spent on Facebook was still a significant predictor of the experience of jealousy," Muise said.

It's a strange concept, but if you want to avoid some of the jealousy in your relationship, you'll have to give Facebook a bit of a rest.

Facebook is addictive

2. It's Too Easy to Reconnect with Ex's

Even though she told you she was still really close with her ex-boyfriend before you started dating, you didn't think you'd be seeing his picture on her wall more than your own! While it may be frustrating, you're not alone. Muise found that over 80 percent of Facebook users add previous romantic or sexual partners. Before Facebook, if your girlfriend wanted to communicate with her ex you didn't have to know about it, now it's there for you and all her other friends to see.

3. It Over-Informs

In this information age not even relationships are spared. Gone are the days when lipstick on the collar was the only sign your mate was being unfaithful. Now the information practically comes to you. All you have to do is to log in. The "tagged" pictures, the "liked" statuses, and the shared plans for this weekend could all potentially trigger feelings of jealousy.

"Facebook is a forum that can expose individuals to more information about their partner than they may otherwise have access to." Muise said. In addition, Facebook allows you to monitor your partner's activities without being detected. With other social networking sites, you'd need a password to see all that Facebook tells you for free.

4. It Appeals to Women, to Their Chagrin

If you think your girlfriend hasn't seen something on your Facebook profile, you're wrong. Not only has she seen it, she's already become enraged, discussed it with her girlfriends and is waiting to confront you about it. Sorry ladies, but those two X chromosomes don't work in your favour when it comes to Facebook. While Muise and her colleagues found that women are not more jealous than men, they did find that women spent more time on Facebook than men. Which means their relationship jealousy was more likely to be ignited by Facebook than a man's.

5. It May Just Be You

Before you blame all of your failed relationships on Facebook, just wait. If you thought your kindergarten girlfriend was cheating on you because she shared her chips with another boy in your class, the green-eyed monster may just reside in your DNA. At the end of the day Muise and her colleagues recognized that other factors like the dynamic of the relationship and one's own propensity towards jealous behaviour could also make them 'Facebook jealous'.

BUT IT IS NOT ONLY THE YOUNGER ONES: THE OLDER ARE ALSO ADDICTED AND MISBEHAVE ON THIS ONLINE SITE.

Now if it was only the younger generation, we could have given them a chance. But we have seen, it is often the elder ones who monger and bicker on online sites. More than revitalizing themselves, they end up harming themselves EMOTIONALLY.

Virtual friendship takes a toll on their lives. People start giving more time to their virtual and nonexistent friends than their existent ones. And sometimes as discussed earlier too, excess of it spoils your current relationship!

I think it is sincerely high time when someone else has to discover something more interesting and alluring than Facebook, so at least the older generation is spared from the virtual world to take care of the younger!

Again I feel a school post the age of thirty is required to groom emotionally.

❋❋

Chapter Twelve

Men And Moments: Reasons Of Rash Behaviour After The Age Of Thirty And Beyond.

There are many factors responsible for the aggressive behaviour of people beyond the age of thirty. Let us evaluate:

1. Fear of Losing

Sitting back quietly reviewing life's upheavals brought me very close to a reality which generally is faced by everyone – reality of aggressiveness. There are moments which give us unlimited pain and simultaneously there are moments which bring to us extreme joy! But it is a plain truth that people in different age groups view 'this phenomenon' in a different light. Here I am trying to pull out those in age group of thirties from a bowl of a hot water and give them a saner platform.

The fear faced by the protagonist, Veronica, in Paulo Coelho's novel '*Veronica Decides To Die*' is nothing new. This fear is faced by majority of us. Whenever good times approach, many of us fear that this might be a temporary phase and that these days won't last long. This one fear is faced by all in all ages. It is not only faced by those in relationships – the same is the case when people face career choices. A burgeoning career with few exceptions has to meet its ebb – a blooming love has to wither and if it does not wither it is preserved using preservatives but the perfume definitely vanishes. Many are not able to take this one truth of life positively, especially those crafting their careers in the age group of thirties going onto 40's-50's!

In the age group of thirties, these days people are generally trying to foster their career……

2. Fear of Loneliness:

Fear of loneliness, to lose someone on the way of life, not to be as successful as others also make people in this age group wild and untamed.

Fear of loneliness

To dream big is good. To work hard to turn dream into reality is also advocated but to be a 'Dreamer' is not at all advocated. Rudyard Kipling too has said, "Dream big but do not make dreams your Master".

Rash behavior/franticness/ fidgetiness leads to mental demolition. This 'mental demolition' takes in its grip not only the life of the person undergoing the turmoil but also his near and dear ones. Their close companions are the first ones to bear the flames of aggressiveness.

NEED OF A SCHOOL TO TAME MOMENTUOUS SPURT OF UNPREDICTABLE BEHAVIOUR.

REASONS OF AGGRESSION:

Can be due to sexless relationships.

Sex is an essential ingredient of a healthy and happy life. But when this is lacking in anyone's life, it is sure that the person is going to react negatively. So we can not negate the importance of sex in a person's healthy life. Relationships which are sexless either result into passivity or extreme aggression. But if at any time, any couple prefers this, they are most welcomed to go ahead but they have to keep in mind that their relationship has to have some zing – some zest and energy involved. Maybe it's a game or a hobby which involves both at the same time. It shouldn't be that one is busy writing and other busy playing cards and all in the name of giving space to each other. A time comes when 'boredom' seeps into this kind of relationship resulting in a final breakdown.

Aggression can sometimes have positive outcomes. For example, it may help a person overcome competition to rise to the top at work. But when aggression is fueled by negative emotions such as anger and when it interferes with life – trouble with the law for fighting, for instance – it is problematic. This type of aggression often has underlying brain pathology.

Definition

There are two general subtypes of aggression. Instrumental aggression is goal oriented and purposeful. Reactive impulsive aggression is typically associated with anger. Reactive aggression typically is considered pathological aggression, referring to hostile, injurious or destructive behaviour caused by frustration.

Source: Livestrong Article.

Why People Get Aggressive In Our Online Community

When people get angry in your community, it's for one of the two reasons. They either want to have greater status in your community or they are worried about losing their current status (it's usually the latter).

Never remove the symptom (the fight) without resolving the cause (individual's feelings). If you want to diffuse aggression you have to remove the fear that what's happening will lose their status.

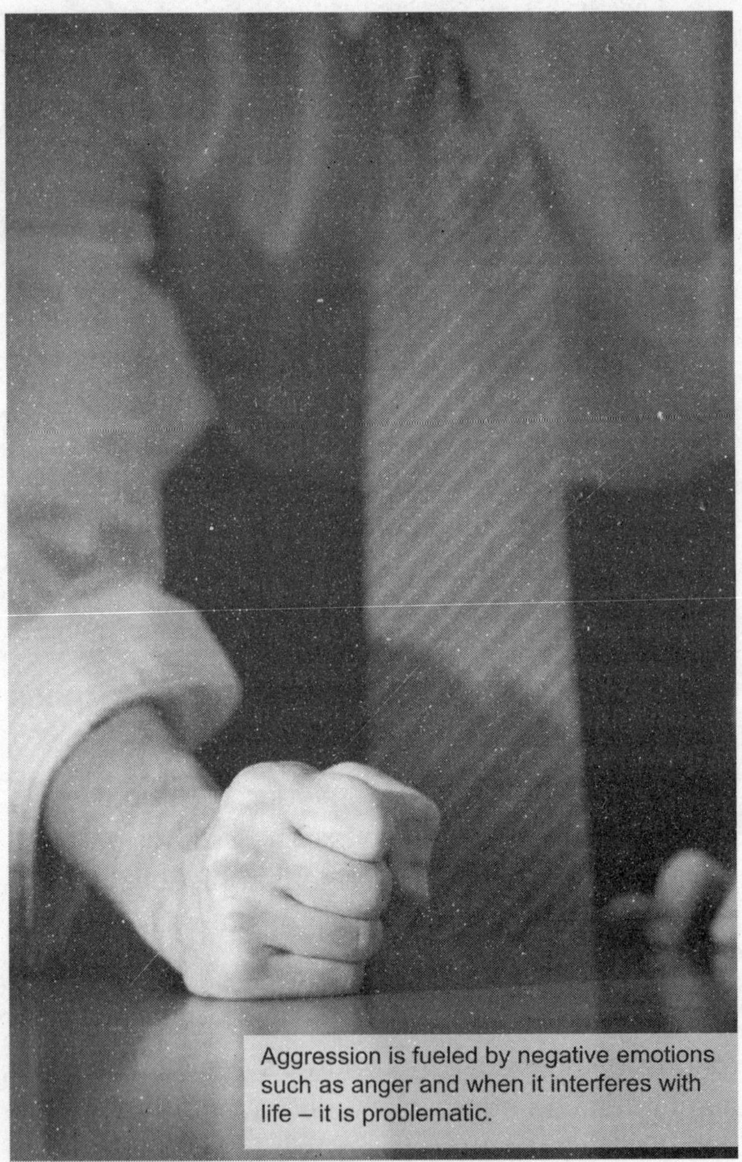
Aggression is fueled by negative emotions such as anger and when it interferes with life – it is problematic.

You can praise or empower members that feel threatened.

If this fails, you can do the threatening. You can remind members that continuing the aggression will result in a loss of status within your community.

Sure some trolls fight for fun and others are naturally aggressive people. But, by far, the majority of the fights in your community can be resolved with simple affirmations and by talking it over, discussing among ourselves and more can be gained by getting along.

We all wish for a psychological aspirin to relieve our worries and pains. We would like someone else to solve the problem of violence in our society. We want the police, the courts, and the prisons to do their jobs and to protect us from criminals. However, there is one area where we can influence aggressive behaviour; that is to learn how to control our own counter aggressive actions.

⁂⁂

Chapter Thirteen

Delhites Excell in Misbehaviour : Mumbaikaars, 'the biggest spitting machine' : Misbehaviour In Middle Age

According to a survey conducted in June 2007 in Delhi, it was found that Delhites are far ahead of other citizens of India in the field of 'MISBEHAVIOUR'

Lack of urbaneness has been found among Delhites with a survey saying many of the denizens excel in spitting, littering, misbehaviour and using abusive language.

The survey on 'Human Behaviour in Public Places', conducted by students of the Anthropology Department of Delhi University, also found that encroachment on roads and other public land was a normal scene in most of the posh market areas in the city.

In Meher Chand Market, close to Lodhi Road in south Delhi, within a span of 40 minutes, the surveyor saw 19 people, including 18 men and a woman, who spat on the road.

Similarly, another student, who surveyed the Chandni Chowk area, came across 49 people spitting in public places. They included 48 men and a woman.

"We have been surveying human behaviour in public places of Delhi for the last three years. We do not find a remarkable change in their attitude," head of the department P C Joshi, under whose guidance the survey was undertaken, said.

The survey was started in 2004 and students of the department visited around 20 localities and observed the behaviour of the people.

In 2005 and 2006, the students selected another 40 localities for the survey.

The findings of the survey in every locality were more or less the same.

Littering was mostly done by middle-aged people, Joshi said.

For example, in Meher Chand market, the surveyors came across 16 people, including nine middle-aged people, who threw away fruit peels, paper, plastic packets and wrappers within an hour's time on a particular day.

In Chandni Chowk, 131 people were seen littering indiscriminately in the market in just half-an-hour. "In fact, there are not enough dustbins in the market area. Besides, littering seems to have become a bad habit of the people," Joshi said.

The common types of misbehaviour are using abusive or unparliamentary language and showing disrespect to women by passing lewd comments, whistling and making vulgar gestures, he said.

The survey found as many as 88 people misbehaving in Chandni Chowk market area within half-an-hour on the day the surveyors visited the place.

Encroachment is common in markets and other public places in the city, Joshi said.

"We did not find any market which is free from encroachment. People extend their houses and shops and encroach upon public space," he said.

The students also interviewed around 100 people in each locality, covering about 2,000 people in a year, and asked them various questions on safety, cleanliness, governance, cost of living and the overall amenities in Delhi.

AND MUMBAIKARS? WHAT DO YOU THINK OF THEM?

MUMBAI: 24 Mar 2012: The city may be in the grip of a virulent strain of the tubercle bacillus, but that has not served as a deterrent to Mumbaikars who, like most Indians, can't help spitting in public. From July to December 2011, Mumbaikars paid around Rs 2.24 crore in fines for spitting, and, the 1.1 lakh people fined is not even the tip of the iceberg.

Every day, lakhs of people get away with this anti-social and harmful habit, say health officials shouting hoarse that TB is spread via droplets released by patients coughing, sneezing or spitting.

Just last week, the Bombay high court observed, "spitting is an inherent characteristic of Indians." But this trait is abetting the spread of TB. The court had made the observation while hearing a petition challenging the power given by Brihanmumbai Municipal Corporation to clean-up marshals to fine offenders. The marshals, who can impose fines of Rs 200, say more often than not, people refuse to pay and simply laugh it off.

Spitting in public places crosses class barriers

Spitting is not confined to any class. It crosses all class barriers.

The Brihanmumbai Municipal Corporation does not categorize fines by the nature of the offence, but an official told TOI that 70% of the fines collected in the Rs 200 category were for spitting. Of the Rs 3.21 crore collected, around Rs 2.24 crore was for spitting.

Tuberculosis, which is spread by spitting and coughing, caused 9,168 deaths in Mumbai last year.

"There are various cleanliness and sanitation bylaws, under which we fine offenders. Spitting in a public place calls for a Rs 200 fine, as also urinating and washing utensils in public. But the last two offences make up only around 30% of the offenders," said a civic official.

Another malaise with Indians is the habit of chewing pan, tobacco or pan masala, all of which require spitting. This spraying of saliva in the public domain crosses class barriers, say experts, though it is more predominant in the lower middle class. "I was standing in Bandra when a Rolls Royce Phantom pulled up in front of us. The person in the back seat rolled down the window, and spat out a huge gob of pan. It was not the driver, but the owner," said executive Rakshit Mehra.

Anisha Shah (25) as part of her college project, she and her team took it upon themselves to stop people who spat in public. "When we tried to inform people about the danger of this anti-social habit, they would either walk away or shrug," said Shah.

Now after going through all the above examples as meticulously observed by the survey, and cited by PTI, anyone can conclude that it is mainly the middle aged people emerging as the new brand of ruffians on the road with their rustic behaviour.

SOURCES:

PTI. JUNE 2007

The Economic Times.

❋❋

Chapter Fourteen

PERFECTIONISM: THIRTY AND BEYOND

Another deadly insect eating away mankind is the importance attached to'Perfectionism'. Now one can ask, how perfectionism can be negative. To be perfect is good. But to be 'over-perfect' can be killing. Perfectionism in a way becomes a disease. Perfectionists do not enjoy their lives and make the lives of those near them miserable as well.

Perfectionism, in psychology, is a belief that perfection should be strict.

But if seen closely, perfectionism can be very damaging.

In its pathological form, it is an unhealthy belief that anything less than perfect is unacceptable.

Perfectionism can drive people to accomplishments and provide the motivation to persevere in the face of discouragement and obstacles.

Adaptive perfectionists have lower levels of procrastination than non-perfectionists. High-achieving athletes, scientists, and artists often show signs of perfectionism. For example, Michelangelo's perfectionism may have spurred him to create masterpieces such as David and the Sistine Chapel.

Perfectionism is associated with giftedness in children. In its pathological form.

But if seen closely, perfectionism can be very damaging. And this kind of Perfectionism is mainly seen in people in age group of post thirty.

It can take the form of procrastination when it is used to postpone tasks ("I can't start my project until I know the 'right' way to do it"), and self-deprecation when it is used to excuse poor performance or to seek sympathy and affirmation from other people.

In the workplace, perfectionism is often marked by low productivity as individuals lose time and energy on small irrelevant details of larger projects or mundane daily activities.

OLDER PERFECTIONISTS

The most dangerous example of Perfectionism is found in the people beyond the age of thirty.

The negative attitude related to their Perfectionism is that they do not even realize that they are in fact being continuously 'a nagging creature' for their near and dear ones.

David D. Burns is an adjunct professor emeritus in the Department of Psychiatry and Behavioral Sciences at the Stanford University School of Medicine and the author of the best-selling book *Feeling Good: The New Mood Therapy* has very aptly highlighted the above phenomenon.

In today's world, with pressure to do and achieve everything, who doesn't want to be a Superwoman or a Superman? All of us want and feel the need to be perfect. But being a perfectionist is debilitating because we feel, each and every day, like we don't measure up – we are not up to the mark and then we land up breaking ourselves.

I know a lady post the age of thirty, who always wanted her home to be perfect. She wanted her children, her husband, her dog, her office to be perfect. In fact she wanted everything in her life to be perfect and in a bid to do so she lost the warmth of all her relationships. Even her dog would no more run after her with love as she was continually nagging him with different rules. The quest of her perfectionism in a way hindered her to achieve more and enjoy life in the process.

This woman Trishla (name changed), a friend of mine became a pain in the neck for her family members. Her own children hated her presence in the house. The situation became so difficult for her family members that she had to be taken to the Psychiatrist. Here Trishla however agreed visiting the Psychiatrist as she too felt that she, somewhere on the path of life has lost her lovely and valuable relationships. But there are many who are stubborn to the hilt and do not want to be taken

A perfectionist can be a pain in the neck for his/her family

to the doctor as they feel 'they are perfect and do not need any help!'

Hence I believe that feel good factor is very important for a healthy life and perfectionism can never make space for this aspect. A perfectionist is in a constant state of unhappiness as he is never satisfied with his own work, or with those with whom he is working.

He is unhappy with his toilet – the shape, size and cleanliness of it and the same time he is unhappy with his children – their achievements which never measure upto his expectations! Now isn't this something mind boggling? It really drains me out when I think how people in quest of achieving perfectionism lose their relationships and happy living.

The middle-age requires peace. This peace of mind can be achieved by adhering to a middle path. This is life. There are ups and down everywhere. Sometimes you can be upset because your maid has not arrived and sometimes you cannot see your boss eye to eye.

The perfectionist in us cannot only hamper our mental peace but also our physical health. As in a bid to make everything look perfect we sometimes go to such limits which is not advisable. People above the age of thirty are prone to High Blood Pressure risks and it is here that they have to decide to stay away from Perfectionism leading to 'Hyper Tension'.

⁂⁂

Epilogue

Second Chance

It knocked at my door

Silently

I tiptoed to it

Hushingly

I smiled at it

Knowingly

It looked once again at me

Lovingly

It stretched its arms

Longingly

I gave it a second chance

Understandingly!

Well, I hope you all have understood the purpose of this book. Life is unpredictable and does not always come the way, in which we want. But, yes, we can always mould it in the way we desire. It is never too late.

Let us take some examples from our prestigious film industry. Many successful actors are able to mould themselves with the changing times and many are not. Those who could adjust and adapt themselves to the 'changing times' are still shining as a bright star, like our favourite Amitabh Bachchan. He was a superstar 'yesterday' and a superstar even 'today'. This is possible because he realized that he can do lead roles suitable to his age. And he excelled in it. He realized the effects of 'changing time' and cautiously adapted himself to it. In fact before switching to character roles, he tried his hands in a couple of 'macho' kind of hero oriented films like 'Jadugar' etc but they failed. It was probably here this Icon realized that 'time and tide leaves none' and very deftly bowed in front of it. I wished many others too would have done so.

I remember a yesterday's successful heroine, according to the newspapers, going berserk as she could not stage a comeback on the platform of life. Her love and professional life, both came heavy upon her and she found herself broken. Her beauty had evaporated and she was afraid to see herself in the mirror.

Sylvia Plath in the poem '*The Mirror*' has beautifully examined and exposed the fear of middle aged people. According to me '*The Mirror*' initially represents childhood – as children, we say whatever is on our minds. Children have no preconceptions because they have no evil in them. They do not judge. Yet, they are capable of saying, "You look horrible today," because to them that is the truth. In their minds, they are not being rude; they are just being truthful.

As we grow older, harsh experiences affect us. Sylvia Plath's father died when she was a young girl. That had a tremendous impact on her, perhaps killing her innocence. Sylvia Plath also attempted suicide when she was in college. That experience

Plath eventually finished her life in her mid thirties as she was unable to handle the pressures of life.

was captured in the autobiographical novel, '*The Bell Jar*'. Sylvia Plath suffered from depression and that lack of mental stability is clearly represented in her poem. Her husband abandoned her in winter with her two children, penniless and powerless, which eventually led to her suicide. To be a genius, sometimes one has to be a bit "crazy." BUT BEING CRAZY DOESN'T MEAN WE HAVE TO BE RUINOUS! Plath eventually finished her life in her mid thirties as she was unable to handle the pressures of life.

Amitabh Bachchan realized thc effects of 'changing time' and cautiously adapted himself to it.

So, though we do agree that Plath was a great Poetess but we have to agree this too that the MID AGE CRISiS TOOK A TOLL ON HER LIFE!

So it is in this age we/you have to guard ourselves from the enemies hidden in us – in our souls. We have to find the best possible remedy or solution for this crisis and actually agree that we are sick!

As reported by Seema Sinha, TOI Reporter in TOI, 27th August 2010, 'Traditionally believed to strike in the 40's now mid-life crisis hits both men and women in the mid-30's. With many careers on a fast track, individuals tend to "burn out" earlier these days and are suddenly faced with crises earlier in life. It begins with individuals questioning their objectives in life and realizing that they have been chasing the wrong goals which has been causing more stress than a sense of well-being and happiness. Sometimes this is compounded by a diminished sex drive as well as a sense of physical and psychological aging'.

She has further added 'A 38-year-old successful businessman felt vulnerable when his colleague died of a sudden heart attack at the age of 36. His grief compounded into depression and he could not come to terms with his own mortality. He decided to live "life to the fullest" which involved a futile relationship with his young secretary and splurging on unnecessary items. All this only compounded his problems including a marital crisis'

The article has also seen quoting, Dr Harish Shetty. According to him "First kiss, sex, addictions, heart attacks... everything's happening early, pre-poning mid-life crisis by eight to 10 years."

So as many Psychologists opine, 'The definition of mid-life has definitely changed over the years. It can happen around 45, at 35, or not until 55. It depends upon how you plan your career and manage your life. It is in our hands to let a mid-life crisis remain a mere psychological term rather than have it affect our lives'.

Actually I feel 'They have achieved all that they set out to, but are still not happy, and scared that they will never be. They crave a change, but don't know what and then this craving many a times lead them to disastrous relationship like multiple extra marital relationships and broken commitments'.

So get up and analyze the pros and cons – See where actually you are trapped and look for ways to make a life and not living!

⁂⁂